Phonics Focus: long e (ea)

THE FEAST

BY CHRISTINA EARLEY
ILLUSTRATED BY
ANASTASIA KLECKNER

A Blue Marlin Book

Introduction:

Phonics is the relationship between letters and their sounds. It is the foundation for reading words, or decoding. A phonogram is a letter or group of letters that represent a sound. Students who practice phonics and sight words become fluent word readers. Having word fluency allows students to build their comprehension skills and become skilled and confident readers.

Activities:

BEFORE READING

Use your finger to underline the key phonogram in each word in the Words to Read list on page 3. Then, read the word. For larger words, look for ways to break the word into smaller parts (double letters, word I know, ending, etc.).

DURING READING

Use sticky notes to annotate for understanding. Write questions, make connections, summarize each page after it is read, or draw an emoji that describes how you felt about different parts.

AFTER READING

Share and discuss your sticky notes with an adult or peer who also read the story.

Key Word/Phonogram: feast

Words to Read:

Bea	teak	beagle
beans	team	beaver
eat	year	Chelsea
heaves	beach	creamy
leap	clean	eager
leaves	dream	Keagan
meal	each	peacock
meat	east	peanut
peace	feast	reason
Peal	gleam	seafood
peas	Heath	season
reads	peach	teapot
sea	screams	upbeat
seal	sneaks	weasel
seat	steams	
tea	treat	

It is the fall season.

This is the time of year when the Peal family eats a big feast for Thanksgiving.

The meal is at Nana and Pop-Pop's home in the east near the sea.

It takes a team to cook this feast!

Bea reads directions for the baked beans. Keagan steams the seafood.

Chelsea heaves the turkey out of the oven. Heath sneaks a treat of meat to Peanut the beagle.

Everyone takes a seat at the teak table.

There is a gleam in each person's eyes. They are eager to eat!

The table is set with beans, seafood, green peas, creamy mashed potatoes, meats, and peach cobbler.

It has been a good year! Each family member tells a reason they are upbeat.

After the meal, the adults work as a team to clean up.

Keagan takes the children to the beach for a walk. They see a seal leap out of the water. Heath screams like a peacock.

Soon, everyone leaves to go home. There is peace and quiet in the house.

Nana and Pop-Pop drink tea from a teapot. Peanut plays with her toy beaver and weasel.

All dream of next year's big feast.

Quiz:

1. True or false? Many people help make the feast.
2. True or false? The children go for a walk before the meal.
3. True or false? The table is made from wood.
4. How do Nana and Pop-Pop feel at the end? How do you know?
5. What is one character trait that Keagan has? What evidence from the story supports your thinking?

Flip the book around for answers!

Answers:

1. True
2. False
3. True
4. Possible answer: Tired, but thankful. They are drinking tea in the quiet house and thinking about next year.
5. Possible answer: Thoughtful, because he takes the kids on a walk so the adults can clean up after the meal.

Activities:

1. Write a story about your favorite big meal or favorite food.

2. Write a new story using some or all of the "ea" words from this book.

3. Create a vocabulary word map for a word that was new to you. Write the word in the middle of a paper. Surround it with a definition, illustration, sentence, and other words related to the vocabulary word.

4. Make a song to help others learn the long e sound of "ea."

5. Design a game to practice reading and spelling words with "ea."

Written by: Christina Earley
Illustrated by: Anastasia Kleckner
Design by: Rhea Magaro-Wallace
Editor: Kim Thompson
Educational Consultant: Marie Lemke, M.Ed
Series Development: James Earley

Library of Congress PCN Data
The Feast (ea) / Christina Earley
Blue Marlin Readers
ISBN 979-8-8873-5000-4 (hard cover)
ISBN 979-8-8873-5059-2 (paperback)
ISBN 979-8-8873-5118-6 (EPUB)
ISBN 979-8-8873-5177-3 (eBook)
Library of Congress Control Number: 2022944992

Printed in the United States of America.

Seahorse Publishing Company
seahorsepub.com

Copyright © 2024 **SEAHORSE PUBLISHING COMPANY**

All rights reserved. No part of this publication may be reproduced, stored in a retrieval system or be transmitted in any form or by any means, electronic, mechanical, photocopying, recording, or otherwise, without the prior written permission of Seahorse Publishing Company.

Published in the United States
Seahorse Publishing
PO Box 771325
Coral Springs, FL 33077